It's My State!

WYOMING

The Equality State

Rick Petreycik and Alicia Klepeis

Cavendish Square

New York

Published in 2016 by Cavendish Square Publishing, LLC
243 5th Avenue, Suite 136, New York, NY 10016

Library of Congress Cataloging-in-Publication Data

Petreycik, Rick, author.
Wyoming / Rick Petreycik and Alicia Klepeis.
pages cm. — (It's my state!)
Includes index.
ISBN 978-1-6271-3259-6 (hardcover) — ISBN 978-1-6271-3261-9 (ebook)
1. Wyoming—Juvenile literature. I. Klepeis, Alicia, 1971- author. II. Title.

F761.3.P48 2016
978.7—dc23

2015032395

Editorial Director: David McNamara
Editor: Fletcher Doyle
Copy Editor: Rebecca Rohan
Art Director: Jeffrey Talbot
Designer: Amy Greenan
Senior Production Manager: Jennifer Ryder-Talbot
Production Editor: Renni Johnson
Photo Research: J8 Media

WYOMING ★ ★ ★ ★
CONTENTS

A QUICK LOOK AT

STATEHOOD: JULY 10, 1890

⭐ State Flower: Indian Paintbrush

The Indian paintbrush was officially named Wyoming's flower on January 31, 1917. The Indian paintbrush has small, green-colored flowers surrounded by colorful leaves. These leaves can be red, orange, yellow, or white. The combination of the leaves and the greenish flowers makes it appear as though the plant has been dipped in a bucket of paint.

⭐ State Bird: Western Meadowlark

The western meadowlark is a songbird with an unmistakable flutelike chirp. The feathers on its wings and back are a mix of brown and white. The feathers along its chest are a bright yellow, with a distinctive V-shaped black mark beneath its throat. It became the state bird on February 5, 1927.

⭐ State Tree: Plains Cottonwood

Cottonwoods can be found along Wyoming's streams and rivers, especially in the eastern part of the state. Some cottonwoods grow to be more than 100 feet (30.5 meters) high. Their thick, rough-textured leaves make a rattling sound when the wind stirs them. The plains cottonwood was first adopted as the state tree in 1947.

WYOMING
★ ★ ★ ★
POPULATION: 563,626

★ State Mammal: **Bison**

Bison, which are also known as buffalo, once roamed the Great Plains in large herds. Bison in the wild had nearly vanished by the start the twentieth century because of overhunting. However, thanks to programs and laws, today the number of bison has increased. A wild herd can be seen in Wyoming's Yellowstone National Park.

★ State Dinosaur: **Triceratops**

About seventy-two to sixty-five million years ago, this rhinoceros-like, plant-eating dinosaur was quite common in the region. The triceratops had three horns on its face. It also had a large, bony plate extending from the back of its skull. A triceratops's body was about 30 feet (9 m) long and weighed between 6 and 12 tons (5.4–10.8 metric tons).

★ State Insect: **Sheridan's Hairstreak**

The Sheridan's Hairstreak is a type of butterfly. It received the title of Wyoming's official insect in 2009. These small butterflies are distinctive for their brilliant green coloring. They often live in dry environments such as sagebrush scrub. The females lay their eggs in wild buckwheat leaves.

A moose searching for food in a river at the foot of the Grand Tetons shows the wonderful diversity of life and geography in Wyoming.

The Equality State

As the old saying goes, "variety is the spice of life." If variety makes things interesting, then Wyoming is definitely one of the most fascinating states in the nation. The state's land area is about 97,093 square miles (251,470 square kilometers), which makes it the ninth-largest state in the country. Wyoming has breathtaking mountains, red deserts, towering waterfalls, dry plains, bubbling mineral springs, gushing water jets, and spectacular canyons.

Wyoming is located in the western part of the United States. Bordering six other states, Wyoming's shape comes close to resembling a perfect rectangle. From east to west, the state measures 364 miles (586 kilometers), and its distance from north to south is about 276 miles (444 km). Wyoming's unique geography consists of three major landforms: plains, mountains, and basins.

Wyoming Borders	
North:	Montana
South:	Utah
	Colorado
East:	Nebraska
	South Dakota
West:	Idaho
	Utah
	Montana

The flat prairies of Wyoming provide grazing grounds for cattle and other livestock.

The Great Plains

Most of eastern Wyoming is a high, somewhat treeless area that is broken up by low foothills, mountains, and occasional buttes, which are flat-topped, tall hills. Eastern Wyoming is part of the Great Plains region. In fact, Wyoming takes its name from an Algonquian word meaning "large prairie place." This region is a high plateau that extends diagonally downward from northwestern Canada all the way to Texas. On average, the elevation of this area ranges from about 5,000 to 6,000 feet (1,524 to 1,829 m).

The area was once covered with tall grasses. Today, the plains in Wyoming serve as excellent grazing land for cattle and sheep. Most of the area is too dry to grow a variety of crops. However, underground **irrigation** systems—which bring water to dry areas— have allowed farmers in some areas to produce corn, sugar beets, barley, hay, beans, and potatoes. Cheyenne, Wyoming's capital city, is located in this region. With a population of about 59,466, Cheyenne is Wyoming's largest city.

The Mountains

Wyoming is home to a number of sweeping mountain ranges. Three-quarters of the state lies more than 1 mile (1.6 km) high in elevation. In fact, Wyoming's land surface has an average elevation of 6,700 feet (2,042 m) above sea level. This is higher than all the other states except Colorado.

In the northeastern corner of the state and extending into South Dakota are the Black Hills. These are a series of low mountains that average about 6,000 feet (1,829 m) high. A well-known point of interest within the area surrounding the Black Hills is Devils Tower, a 1,267-foot (386 m) butte that resembles a gigantic tree stump. Although the Black Hills are a relatively dry area, they are covered with ponderosa pines, which give the hills a darkish appearance when viewed from a distance.

To the south of Wyoming's high grassy plains are the Laramie Mountains. These mountains stretch across the state for about 140 miles (225 km). Near the northern section of the Laramie Mountains and almost in the center of Wyoming is Casper. This is the state's main oil-producing city. During the winter months, people who like to ski travel to Casper from all around the United States to enjoy the area's many fine, snow-powdered slopes. In the summer, Casper is also a popular destination for swimmers and boaters. Nearby Pathfinder, Alcova, and Seminoe reservoirs are perfect for enjoying water-sports activities.

To the west of Wyoming's Great Plains is a series of jagged mountain ranges that are part of the majestic Rocky Mountain chain. The Rockies extend from Canada all the way to Mexico. Wyoming's portion of the Rocky Mountains includes the Sierra Madre and Medicine Bow Mountains in the south; the Bighorn, Wind River, and Absaroka Ranges in the north; and the Gros Ventre, Salt River, Snake River, and Teton Ranges in the west. Western Wyoming is also home to the state's highest mountain, Gannett Peak, which rises 13,804 feet (4,207 m) as part of the Wind River Range.

Wyoming's mountain lakes are ideal for camping and an attractive destination for hikers.

WYOMING
COUNTY MAP

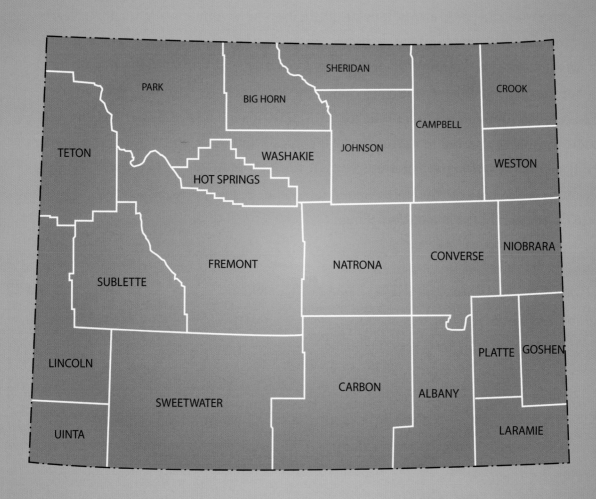

PARK

SHERIDAN

CROOK

BIG HORN

TETON

CAMPBELL

WASHAKIE

JOHNSON

WESTON

HOT SPRINGS

FREMONT

NATRONA

CONVERSE

NIOBRARA

SUBLETTE

LINCOLN

PLATTE

GOSHEN

SWEETWATER

CARBON

ALBANY

UINTA

LARAMIE

WYOMING
POPULATION BY COUNTY

County	Population
Albany County	36,299
Big Horn County	11,668
Campbell County	46,133
Carbon County	15,885
Converse County	13,833
Crook County	7,083
Fremont County	40,123
Goshen County	13,249
Hot Springs County	4,812
Johnson County	8,569
Laramie County	91,738
Lincoln County	18,106
Natrona County	75,450
Niobara County	2,484
Park County	28,205
Platte County	8,667
Sheridan County	29,116
Sublette County	10,247
Sweetwater County	43,806
Teton County	21,294
Uinta County	21,118
Washakie County	8,533
Weston County	7,208

Source: US Bureau of the Census, 2010

Cities such as Casper grew along the lines of the intercontinental railroad.

In the northwestern corner of the state is Yellowstone National Park. Established in 1872, it is the oldest national park in the United States—and the world. The park covers more than 2 million acres (809,371 hectares) and features magnificent mountains, thundering waterfalls, and deep reddish-brown gorges. Yellowstone Lower Falls is located in the park. This is a magnificent waterfall that plunges 308 feet (94 m) into the scenic Grand Canyon of the Yellowstone.

Yellowstone also has about three thousand hot springs and geysers. A geyser is a natural hot spring that shoots a column of water and steam into the air every now and then. The most well-known geyser in Yellowstone is Old Faithful. Every 35 to 120 minutes, it shoots a column of water into the air about 130 feet (40 m) high. The tallest geyser in the park is Steamboat Geyser, which sprays water as high as 400 feet (122 m) in the air. A variety of animals live in the park, including elk, mule deer, moose, bison, black bears, and giant grizzly bears.

In Their Own Words

"In September 1891 ... I made an elk-hunt in northwestern Wyoming among the Shoshone Mountains, where they join the Hoodoo and Absaroka Ranges. There is no more beautiful game country in the United States."
—Theodore Roosevelt

Near the eastern entrance to Yellowstone is the town of Cody, which was named after the famous frontiersman and entertainer William Frederick "Buffalo Bill" Cody. A popular town attraction is the Buffalo Bill Historical Center. Cody also has the Whitney Western Art Museum, the Plains Indian Museum, the Cody Firearms Museum, the Draper Natural History Museum, and the Harold McCracken Research Library.

A ridge of mountains runs back and forth from the northwestern corner of Wyoming all the way down to the state's south-central border. It is called the Continental Divide, and it plays a huge role in directing the flow of rivers along its path. The Continental Divide starts in Alaska, runs through Canada, the United States, and Mexico, and then spans into Central America. Rivers that start west of the Continental Divide flow toward the Pacific Ocean. Rivers that start east of the divide flow toward the Atlantic Ocean and the Gulf of Mexico.

The Basins

Several basins dotted with sagebrush make up Wyoming's third major landform. Basins are deep, bowl-shaped depressions, or "holes" as Wyomingites like to call them. The basins'

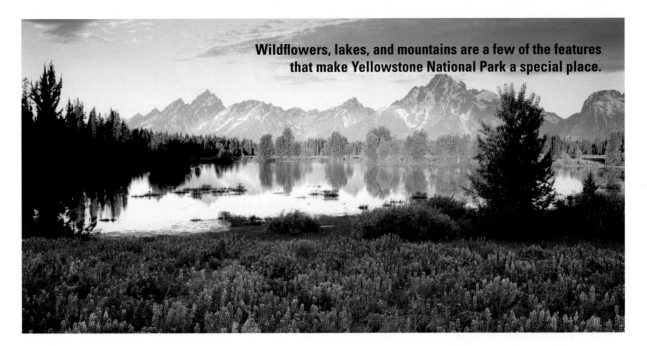
Wildflowers, lakes, and mountains are a few of the features that make Yellowstone National Park a special place.

tops are surrounded by mountains. Some of Wyoming's largest basins include the Washakie, Green River, and Great Divide Basins in the south. The Green River Basin is one of the state's best agricultural areas. Located north of the Sierra Madre Range, the Great Divide Basin is Wyoming's biggest basin, but it is quite high in elevation—higher than the Green River or the Bighorn Basins—and the poorly drained soils and very dry climate make it unsuitable for farming. Sheep and cattle grazing are really the only agricultural activities associated with this area. The Bighorn and Powder River Basins are large basins in the northern part of the state. The Wind River Basin is located in central Wyoming.

West of Casper is the 320-acre (130 ha) Midway Geyser Basin, which is often called Hell's Half Acre. Over a period spanning thousands of years, the constant interaction between wind and water here has created an assortment of eerie-looking ridges, towers, and carved-out gullies. Many feel that these structures look as if they belong on another planet.

Climate

For the most part, Wyoming's climate tends to be cool, sunny, and dry. However, extreme weather conditions in both winter and summer months are not uncommon. For example, it is not unusual for winter temperatures to be a freezing –30 degrees Fahrenheit (–34.4 degrees Celsius). On February 9, 1933, the temperature plummeted to a bone-chilling –66°F (–54.4°C) in the town of Riverside. That went into the record books as the state's all-time low. Wyoming's average January temperature typically varies from 5 to –10°F (–15 to –23.3°C), though in the state's western valleys, the average is a chilly –5°F (–20.6°C).

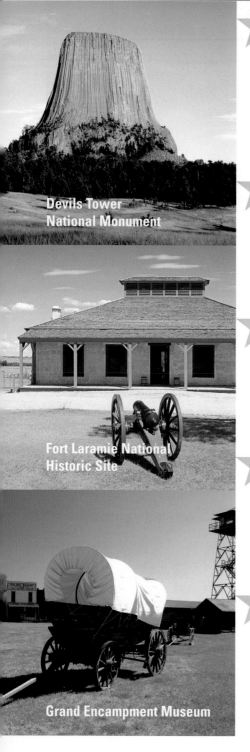

Devils Tower National Monument

Fort Laramie National Historic Site

Grand Encampment Museum

1. Buffalo Bill Museum

Visitors to Cody can learn about the life and times of William F. "Buffalo Bill" Cody, a scout, frontiersman, and actor who lived from 1846 to 1917. The museum also explores the history of the American cowboy, dude ranching, and myths about the American West.

2. Devils Tower National Monument

Rising above the surrounding grassland and ponderosa pine forest near Hulett is this remarkable geologic feature. Made of igneous rock, this stone tower is sacred to the Lakota people and several other Northern Plains tribes.

3. Fort Laramie National Historic Site

Once a military post that protected and supplied settlers, this site offers a glimpse into the past with twelve restored buildings and guided tours. Costumed interpreters help visitors feel they have traveled back in time.

4. Grand Encampment Museum

History buffs will love this museum's buildings, including a schoolhouse, stage station, blacksmith shop, and Forest Service ranger cabins. The museum celebrates the history of the mining, timber, and agricultural industries in Encampment Valley.

5. Grand Teton National Park

Outdoor enthusiasts can hike, bike, and canoe to explore this spectacular park's mountains, valleys, and lakes. There are trails that Native Americans and fur trappers used in the 1820s, campsites, and old ranches and homesteads.

WYOMING ★ ★ ★ ★

6. Hot Springs State Park

Soak in the park's bathhouse where mineral hot springs provide therapeutic waters kept at 104°F (40°C). There are hiking trails, beautiful flower gardens, and bison herds year-round.

7. Killpecker Sand Dunes

Part of the Red Desert near Rock Springs, this is one of America's largest natural sandboxes. A volcanic plug called Boar's Tusk pops out of the ground. Adventure lovers can also ride off-road vehicles across these enormous sand dunes.

8. National Elk Refuge

From December through April, visitors to Jackson can bundle up and take a horse-drawn sleigh ride amidst thousands of elk that are part of the refuge's herd. Fishers will want to catch some of the area's varied trout species.

9. Shoshone Tribal Cultural Center

Explore Fort Washakie to find out more about historical figures including Sacagawea and Chief Washakie. Take a walking tour or look at crafts and historical artifacts from the Shoshone culture.

10. Yellowstone National Park

America's first national park is like another world. It contains half of all the world's known **geothermal** features (including hot springs, mud pots, fumaroles, and travertine terraces) and the world's largest concentration of geysers—more than three hundred, or two-thirds of all those on Earth. It is also home to grizzly bears, wolves, and herds of bison and elk.

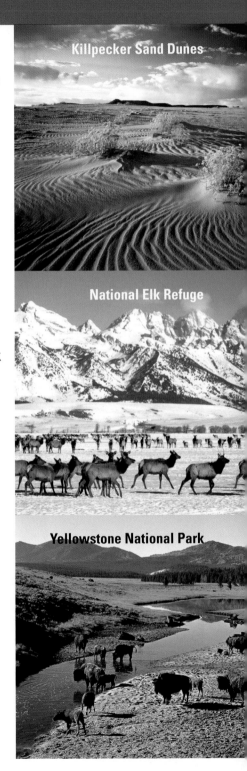

Killpecker Sand Dunes

National Elk Refuge

Yellowstone National Park

Summer temperatures vary, depending upon the area of the state. For example, in the mountainous regions, summers are delightfully cool. On the other hand, temperatures on the low-lying eastern plains can be very hot. Residents of the town of Basin got a taste of just how hot it can get when the temperature soared to a record-breaking 115°F (46.1°C) on July 12, 1900.

When it comes to precipitation—water that falls as either rain, sleet, or snow—Wyoming averages only about 13 inches (33 centimeters) a year, making it a rather dry state. Rainfall is very scarce in the plains and basin areas, but a common phenomenon in the higher-altitude regions. In the mountainous areas, snowfall is also a frequent occurrence, particularly in the Absarokas and Tetons. In fact, it is not uncommon for roads leading to and from both mountain ranges to be completely shut down between October and May. This is because of the ever-present threat of avalanches, which are overwhelming floods of snow that can occur when a snowbank suddenly breaks away from the side of a mountain.

The amount of snow and rain in Wyoming varies greatly by region.

Aspen trees color the hillsides of Wyoming yellow in the fall.

Wildlife

Wyoming's diverse landscape is home to a wide variety of plants and animals. From its mountain ranges to the Great Plains, Wyoming has many **habitats** where plants can live. The state's elevation plays a key role in determining where specific species of trees, plants, and flowers grow. For example, the colder, higher-altitude regions provide a good environment for the growth of mosses, lichens, and evergreen trees such as the Douglas fir and ponderosa pine. Mountain mahoganies thrive in the lower-elevation valleys, as do wildflowers such as buttercups, goldenrods, evening stars, forget-me-nots, and arnicas. Cottonwoods, aspens, willows, and hawthorns, as well as greasewoods, yuccas, and cacti grow in the drier eastern plains. Sagebrush is a hardy plant that can grow in much of Wyoming from the mountainous areas to the state's deserts.

Wyoming is fortunate to have many national forests within its boundaries, including the nation's first, Shoshone National Forest. Located in the northwestern part of the state, Shoshone National Forest's terrain is varied. It houses craggy mountains that are snowcapped all year, as well as plains filled with sagebrush. Tourists often flock to southwestern Wyoming's Medicine Bow-Routt National Forest where they can find large stands of lodgepole pine, as well as aspen, subalpine fir, and Engelmann spruce trees. Sagebrush, Gambel oaks, and the beautiful flowering serviceberry tree live in the sagebrush steppe part of this national forest. In addition, people come to Medicine Bow-Routt National Forest in the summer to rock climb and hike at a spot called Vedauwoo. In the winter, snowmobilers and cross-country skiers favor the area.

Grasses are important plants in Wyoming. Many varieties exist across the state. A few examples include bluegrass, buffalo grass, and wheatgrass. But wildflowers are also found in Wyoming's forests and grasslands. Glacier lilies, lupine, scarlet gilia, Indian paintbrush, and mule ears are just some species found in the Equality State.

With its many landforms and types of natural environments, Wyoming has a rich variety of animal life. In addition to swift pronghorns, there are moose, elk, bighorn sheep, and mule deer. Black bears, skunks, foxes, raccoons, and chipmunks can be found in the wooded areas. Near Wyoming's waterways you may find beavers, minks, and otters. Gophers, ground squirrels, cottontails, jackrabbits, coyotes, black-footed ferrets, prairie dogs, and snowshoe hares often make their homes on the plains.

Many types of birds thrive in Wyoming. These include magpies, juncos, chickadees, lark buntings, Bullock's orioles, long-tailed chats, western mockingbirds, and western meadowlarks. Larger birds that nest on Wyoming land include wild turkeys, sage hens, and pheasants. Birds of prey, such as bald eagles, golden eagles, hawks, and falcons, fly through the Wyoming skies. Waterbirds, such as swans, pelicans, great blue herons, rails, snipes, gulls, and ospreys, are attracted to the state's wetland areas. For example, Canada geese and a variety of ducks have nested along the Green River for centuries. And sage grouse flocks come to this river for water during summertime.

The National Bighorn Sheep Interpretive Center is located in the town of Dubois.

Among the many fish that inhabit Wyoming's rivers, lakes, and streams are bass, grayling, catfish, pike, muskies, walleyes, perch, and several kinds of trout. Many fishermen enjoy spending their days casting for these fish.

Over the years, Wyoming has gone to great lengths to protect its wildlife. For example, in 1912, it set aside 24,700 acres

Wild mustangs roam through some protected areas of Wyoming.

(9,996 ha) of land near Jackson specifically for elk and other large animals. Known as the National Elk Refuge, this land provides food and protection for about 7,500 elk during the winter months, when natural sources of food are scarce. The added value of this large refuge is that it also keeps the elk from foraging, or looking for food, at neighboring farms. Some other animals that live within this preserve are moose, bison, mule deer, bighorn sheep, and badgers. In addition to the National Elk Refuge, Wyoming has six other national wildlife preserves.

Killer Storm

In 1949, a horrendous blizzard blanketed Wyoming, killing seventeen people, fifty-five thousand cattle, and more than one hundred thousand sheep.

The state has also done a lot to protect plants and animals that are in danger of becoming extinct, or no longer existing. For example, an animal that has made a comeback in recent years is the timber wolf. For hundreds of years, the timber wolf roamed through the region. Starting in the few decades before Wyoming became a state, though, many settlers were determined to keep the timber wolf from attacking their livestock. For many years, the wolves were hunted and killed until they were nearly extinct. Beginning in 1995, however, a group of environmentalists reintroduced the timber wolf into Yellowstone National Park. This initiative helped increase the timber wolves' wild populations. This is just one example of how Wyoming's residents treasure their land and all the life living upon it.

Forget-Me-Not

Glacier Lily

Grizzly Bear

1. Black-Footed Ferret

A member of the weasel family, the black-footed ferret is the only ferret native to North America. Once thought to be extinct, these ferrets were rediscovered in 1981 near Meeteetse in north-central Wyoming. Breeding programs are reintroducing them into the wild.

2. Forget-Me-Not

Found primarily in Wyoming's lower-elevation areas, this eye-catching wildflower has clusters of small blue flowers. It grows to a height of between 4 and 12 inches (10.1 to 30.5 cm).

3. Glacier Lily

These bright yellow flowers were first noted by the Lewis and Clark expedition in 1806. They live in many habitats, including montane forests, sagebrush, and alpine meadows. This flower often blooms as nearby snow recedes. This flower's bulbs are a favorite food of grizzly bears.

4. Grizzly Bear

The grizzly's long hairs on its back and shoulders often have white or silver tips, giving the animal a grizzled appearance. More than seven hundred grizzly bears live in or around Yellowstone National Park, and their numbers are increasing.

5. Moose

The moose is the largest member of the deer family. They have large snouts, massive antlers, and a flap of skin—called a bell—hanging from their throats. Moose are very good swimmers and can be seen along rivers and streams in summertime.

6. Mountain Lion

Also known as the cougar, the mountain lion is a member of the cat family. It has a small head and small, rounded, black-tipped ears. An adult male measures about 8 feet (2.4 m) from its head to the tip of its tail.

7. Ponderosa Pine

Named because of its bulk, the ponderosa pine averages between 100 and 160 feet (30 to 49 m) in height. This tree has a distinctive orange-brown bark and dark yellow-green needles. Ponderosa pines commonly live for more than two hundred years.

8. Pronghorn

Related to goats and antelope, these graceful, hoofed animals roam the eastern plains of Wyoming in small herds. North America's fastest animal, they have been clocked at speeds of up to 70 miles an hour (113 kilometers per hour).

9. Sage Grouse

Often compared to domestic chickens, sage grouses were once abundant throughout the West. These brownish-gray birds depend on sagebrush for food, especially during winter. Sage grouse populations have declined dramatically due to development and drought.

10. Sagebrush

Wyoming's "sagebrush seas" provide a nursery area for animals including the pronghorn, mule deer, elk, and golden eagle. Many species that live in sagebrush, like the greater sage-grouse, exist nowhere else on Earth. Some sagebrush plants can live more than 150 years.

Ponderosa Pine

Pronghorn

Sagebrush

Some petroglyphs found in Wyoming are believed to be ten thousand years old.

From the Beginning

Scientists and historians believe Wyoming's first residents were Paleo-Indians. These people likely entered the region by way of the Bering land bridge that connected Siberia (in Asia) to North America. Their descendants gradually moved toward the Rocky Mountains and the Great Plains areas. There, they gathered plants and hunted giant mammoths, bison, and other animals.

These Native Americans were quite skilled at making tools for hunting, too. Near Worland, in the northwestern region of the state, scientists have discovered artifacts including stone arrowheads, spear tips, knives, and axes. These artifacts were near mammoth and bison bones dating back to about 9000 BCE.

Around 7000 BCE, the region's climate began to change. The lack of rainfall caused the grasslands to start drying up. Herds of wild animals, such as deer and bison, moved away. The region's Native Americans, who hunted these animals, followed them. As a result, between 7000 BCE and 5000 BCE, there were hardly any human inhabitants in the area now called Wyoming. That began to change around 4500 BCE, probably because of better climate conditions.

A Shoshone artist painted scenes from a buffalo hunt on a traditional hide.

Over the next few thousand years, small bands of Crow and Shoshone Native Americans started making their way into the region that would become Wyoming. The Arapaho and Cheyenne followed later, as well as groups of Sioux.

The Shoshone settled in the mountainous western region of Wyoming. The Arapaho, Cheyenne, and Sioux favored the grassy areas of the Great Plains in the east. There they made shelters out of branches and prairie grasses. They also used animal hides to build conical-shaped dwellings called tepees. Other groups that eventually appeared in what would become Wyoming were the Nez Perce, the Gros Ventre, the Bannock, the Kiowa, and the Flatheads.

Rather than settling down in a permanent spot, all of these Native American groups tended to be **nomadic**. They moved with the seasons, following animals like deer and bison. They also gathered wild fruits and vegetables and fished in the region's waterways.

Horses had a huge effect on the region's Native Americans. Horses were introduced in the early sixteenth century by Spanish explorers and **missionaries** living in the region that would become New Mexico. Many of these horses escaped and started living in the wild. The Native Americans captured and trained them to easily move people and supplies. The horses were also useful when Native Americans hunted or warred with other groups. Over time, the Sioux and Cheyenne gained great power in the region because they possessed large numbers of horses. Because of their use of horses, the Sioux and Cheyenne were able to force less-powerful Native American groups to move away from the best hunting grounds.

New Arrivals

At the beginning of the 1700s, furs were extremely popular in Europe and in North America's growing settlements. Fur was used to make clothing and accessories such as blankets. In 1742, Sieur de La Vérendrye, a French-Canadian military officer, fur trader, and explorer wanted to find a trading route to the Pacific Ocean. He sent his sons on an expedition that brought them into the region that is now northeastern Wyoming. In 1743, the two brothers saw the Bighorn Mountains but decided to turn back.

When the brothers returned home to Manitoba, Canada, their stories about the region's fur-bearing animals—the beaver, fox, mink, and otter—stirred the curiosity of other French trappers and explorers. Over the next sixty years, a few adventurous fortune-seekers from French Canada made their way into what is now Wyoming. They often got along with the Native Americans in the region and learned the native languages and customs. Some married Native American women.

Sacagawea, who served as an interpreter for Lewis and Clark, was a member of the Shoshone tribe.

The Native People

Native people had been living in the territory that is now Wyoming for many thousands of years before European settlers arrived. Many of these early residents were hunters and gatherers who moved in search of food sources. People from the Arapaho, Cheyenne, Crow, Kiowa, Shoshone, Sioux, and Ute tribes were just some of the Native Americans here when European settlers came to the area now called Wyoming.

Generations of Arapaho women live together on the Wind River Indian Reservation.

Wyoming's early Native American tribes had a lot in common with each other. These people were mainly nomadic. They often lived in relatively small groups. They ranged the area's vast plains to find food. Of particular interest were the freely roaming herds of bison. The Native Americans ate the bison meat. They also used the animal hides for clothing and to build their tepees. The Wind River Shoshones also hunted pronghorn, especially in the Wind River and Grand Teton Mountains. Various tribes, including the Crow and Cheyenne, expanded their diet by gathering and eating wild fruits and vegetables as they traveled.

After the Europeans arrived, the lives of the Native Americans definitely changed. There were some friendly relations and trading transactions between the Native Americans and the newly arrived settlers during the early 1800s, but tensions grew as more settlers arrived and took away land. The Dawes General Allotment Act, which broke up large reservations and gave land to individual Native American families, was passed in 1887. It was intended to help Native Americans become farmers and integrate into white society. Nomadic tribes could not adjust to being farmers, though, and much of their land was taken over by white farmers. More than one-third of the land owned by tribes, including some belonging to those in Wyoming, was lost by 1900. Many of the Native Americans had to move to other places.

Today, two federally recognized Native American tribes live in Wyoming: the Eastern Shoshone and the Northern Arapaho. The majority of these Native Americans live on the gigantic Wind River Indian Reservation, located in the west central part of the state. More than 3,900 Eastern Shoshone and 8,600 Northern Arapaho tribal members call this reservation home. The Crow live on a reservation in Montana that borders Wyoming.

Spotlight on the Northern Arapaho

Arapaho is pronounced "uh-RAP-uh-ho." It comes from the Crow word *alappahó*, which means "many tattoo marks." The Northern Arapaho were known as buffalo hunters, brave warriors, and successful raiders among the Plains Native Americans.

Distribution: Today, the Northern Arapaho occupy the Wind River Indian Reservation (along with the Eastern Shoshone), which encompasses over 2 million acres (809,371 ha). The group has around 8,600 members in Wyoming, and their main communities are in Arapahoe, St. Stephens, and Ethete.

Homes: Traditionally, the Northern Arapaho lived in moveable, cone-shaped tepees. These were typically made from wooden poles and buffalo hides. They used buffalo hides for seating and bedding inside their homes.

Food: The staple of the Northern Arapaho diet was bison meat. It could be prepared in different ways, including stews and soups where wild vegetables and fruits were added to the meat. People also made a dish called pemmican by mixing dried buffalo meat, fat, and berries. This was hardy enough to last through the winter.

Clothing: Northern Arapaho men and women wore clothes made of softened deerskin or bison skin. They wore soft moccasins on their feet. Women typically wore leggings under their long dresses. Men wore leggings, shirts, and loincloths or breechcloths. They sometimes decorated their clothing with paint, porcupine quills, and elaborate beadwork.

Art: The Northern Arapaho, like many other Native American peoples of the region, created beautiful beadwork. Sometimes the beads were used to decorate clothing. Northern Arapaho people also often decorated their tepees with colorful paintings.

In 1803, the United States doubled its size when it purchased the Louisiana Territory from France. President Thomas Jefferson hoped to find a water route to the Pacific Ocean. He commissioned Meriwether Lewis and William Clark to lead an expedition into the large unknown territory. Although they never entered the area that would become Wyoming, Lewis and Clark did enlist the services of Sacagawea, a Shoshone woman from the region. She served as their guide and interpreter.

On the return trip, a man named John Colter left the Lewis and Clark expedition. He spent the next four years exploring the northern Rocky Mountains, including the Grand Tetons. In 1807, he discovered both the Jackson Hole and Yellowstone regions.

The Fur Trade Grows

By the early 1800s, consumers from New York to Paris were willing to pay a lot of money for cloaks and hats made from fur-bearing animals, particularly beavers. Owners of fur-trading companies were challenged to get their furs to market as quickly as possible. John Jacob Astor, a wealthy New York businessman, owned the American Fur Company. In 1811, he asked his agent, Wilson Hunt Price, to take command of a trading post being built at the mouth of the Columbia River.

John Jacob Astor built a financial empire around the fur trade.

In 1812, Price sent Robert Stuart eastward to deliver some important messages to Astor. During this journey, Stuart discovered a 20-mile-wide (32 km) opening through the Rocky Mountains. The passageway, which became known as South Pass, played a huge role in boosting the fur industry. It reduced the time it took to deliver animal pelts to markets. It also allowed trappers to hunt in newer, untapped areas.

The everyday lives of trappers and fur traders were extremely dangerous and lonely. These "mountain men" practiced their craft in unexplored territory, withstanding bitter winters and dangerous animals like mountain lions and grizzly bears. These men could go an entire year without seeing another human being.

A trader named William Henry Ashley helped change that sense of isolation in the summer of 1825. He set up a spot at Henry's Fork of the Green River where the mountain men could trade with one another and stock up on supplies. Their meetings evolved into a yearly summertime event that became known as a rendezvous, which also attracted local Native Americans. The participants feasted, sang, danced, played cards, and raced horses. They traded furs for gunpowder, knives, alcohol, tools, firearms, and other goods. Many exchanged information about newly discovered plants, animals, and trails.

In 1834, trappers William Sublette and Robert Campbell set up the Fort William trading post. Here, mountain men could trade and replenish supplies more frequently. Located on the North Platte River, this post became another chief meeting place for trappers and Native Americans.

By the early 1840s, however, the fur trade was about to end. Widespread trapping had nearly wiped out the region's beaver population. Consumers' tastes in fashion also began to shift from hats made from beaver fur to hats made of silk.

Westward Movement

In the mid-1830s, many people in the United States began heading westward. They had heard tales of rolling hills, fertile fields, and pleasant weather along the Pacific Coast. Some sought opportunity; others just craved change.

Missionaries were among the first to journey west. By 1840, more and more people began moving west to what is now Oregon and California. Missionaries and adventure seekers alike had to trek 250 miles (402 km) across Wyoming. The fortune seekers, known as forty-niners, headed toward California after the 1849 gold rush. Their route followed the North Platte and Sweetwater Rivers before crossing the Rockies at South Pass.

Despite the number of people passing through, the land that is now Wyoming was not a place where people wanted to

Close Encounter

Devils Tower was featured in the 1977 science fiction movie *Close Encounters of the Third Kind*, directed by Steven Spielberg.

Making a Native American Rattle

A number of Native American groups in Wyoming have historically made rattles. These noisemakers are often used in traditional tribal ceremonies. Materials used to make these rattles vary widely and have included items such as seashells, turtle shells, bird beaks, seedpods, bones, and even animal hooves. You can use your rattle to make music or to decorate your room.

What You Need

Yarn or twine

A sturdy Y-shaped twig

Scissors

Double-sided tape

Beads, buttons, feathers, shells, and other natural items with a hole in them

A hole puncher (optional, to make holes in objects, if desired)

What To Do

- Cut a few short strips of double-sided tape and wind these at intervals along the twig. This will help the yarn or twine to stay in place as you wrap it.
- Wind the yarn or twine around your Y-shaped twig, covering it completely. It's a good idea to tie a knot (or tape if easier) at the beginning so that the yarn doesn't come unraveled as you work. While you are winding the yarn or twine, feel free to add some decorations along the way, such as a bead or a feather. Fasten the feather by placing its quill between the stick and the yarn or twine.
- Cut another piece of yarn or twine that is 5 to 7 inches (13 to 18 centimeters) longer than the distance between the Y-shaped ends of your twig. Tie one end of this piece of twine to one end of the twig. As you wish, thread some beads, washers, seashells, or other small objects onto the twine. Finally, tie the remaining end of the yarn or twine onto the other arm of your twig.
- Gently swing your rattle and listen for what kinds of sounds it makes. You can also use it as a bedroom decoration.

Deep ruts left by wagons on the Oregon Trail can still be seen clearly.

settle. Some felt the land was too bleak and treeless or too mountainous.

As people headed west, they passed through Native American hunting grounds. Settlers killed many wild animals that the Native people depended on for food. This angered the Native Americans. As a result, many Natives began attacking the newcomers and their wagon trains.

US Army scout and explorer Lieutenant John Charles Frémont told the Congress that the settlers needed protection. So in 1846, Congress authorized the US Army to send troops to the region and build forts along the Oregon Trail. In 1849, military officials turned the trading post of Fort William—in present-day southeastern Wyoming—into an important military post. They renamed it Fort Laramie.

The forts that sprang up along the Oregon Trail beginning in the late 1840s provided protection for settlers heading west. The forts also served as commercial activity centers, where merchants sold flour, sugar, building materials, and other goods.

In 1851, in an attempt to end Native American attacks on the settlers, the US Congress authorized holding a treaty council with the Native Americans of the Great Plains region. About ten thousand Sioux, Cheyenne, Arapaho, Crow, and Shoshone met with D.D. Mitchell (Superintendent of Indian Affairs), Thomas Fitzpatrick (fur trapper and Indian Agent of the Sioux), and US military commanders at the mouth of Horse Creek on the Platte River. There, representatives from all parties signed what came to be known as the Treaty of Fort Laramie.

According to the terms of the treaty, the Native Americans agreed not to attack the new white settlers and to keep peace among themselves. The Native Americans also

The largest steam locomotive in the world, nicknamed *Big Boy*, is on display in the city of Cheyenne.

permitted forts and roads to be built on their lands. In return, the treaty commissioners agreed to pay the natives $50,000 a year for the next fifty years. This was supposed to pay for the damage the newcomers had done to the bison population and their grazing land.

However, Congress soon changed its mind about the $50,000 figure and reduced it to $10,000. Some Native groups were never paid at all. This was one of many agreements with Native Americans that were broken by the US government during the next thirty-five years.

In 1854, a white settler complained that a party of Sioux warriors had killed his stray cow. The army sent Lieutenant John Grattan and twenty-nine soldiers to a Sioux village near Fort Laramie to find the people who had supposedly committed the crime. They asked the Sioux leaders to hand over the guilty individuals. When the Sioux refused, shots were exchanged between the soldiers and the Native Americans. In the confusion that followed, Chief Brave Bear was killed. The Sioux retaliated by killing Grattan and all of his men.

Red Cloud's War ended after these negotiations produced the Treaty of Fort Laramie in 1868.

Conflicts with the Native Americans increased as more white settlers arrived in Wyoming.

As relations between whites and Wyoming's Native Americans worsened, the American Civil War erupted in 1861. No Civil War battles were fought on Wyoming soil. However, the US Army had to pull troops from its Wyoming forts to fight for the Union back east. This left many westward-bound travelers unprotected, and Native American attacks on the wagon trains increased.

In 1862, gold was discovered in Montana. A fortune-seeker from Georgia named John Bozeman cut a trail from Colorado to the Montana gold fields. It ran right through Wyoming's Powder River Basin. This region was prime hunting ground for the Sioux, Arapaho, and Cheyenne. All three groups, especially the Sioux, were angry. Their attacks became more frequent. In 1866, the US Army built Fort Reno and Fort Phil Kearny in northeastern Wyoming.

Between 1865 and 1867, some of the bloodiest battles between Native American warriors and US troops were fought on Wyoming's plains. By 1868, Chief Red Cloud of the Sioux had had enough and was willing to negotiate. A second treaty was signed at Fort Laramie. According to its terms, the Bozeman Trail, as well as Fort Reno, Fort Phil Kearny, and two other forts were closed. It was also agreed that no whites would be allowed to enter the land north of the North Platte River and east of the Bighorn Mountains. In addition, the Sioux and Cheyenne stated they would not stand in the way of a railroad being built across southern Wyoming.

★ 10 ★ KEY CITIES ★ ★ ★

Laramie

Gillette

1. Cheyenne: population 59,466

Wyoming's state capital is both a legislative and a business center. It hosts numerous events from Oktoberfest to the Kids Cowboy Festival each year. Giant, 8-foot-tall (2.4 m tall) cowboy boots, painted and designed by local artists, are scattered throughout the city.

2. Casper: population 55,316

From its early days as a frontier outpost, Casper has developed into a cultural center. Today it's known as Wyoming's Adventure Capital, where water and winter sports entertain visitors.

3. Laramie: population 30,816

Laramie is a great mix of modern and old. Its historic sites and museums offer a glimpse into its past, but its excellent university and downtown are twenty-first century. Shoppers, foodies, and sports lovers will all have fun in this vibrant city.

4. Gillette: population 29,087

This city in northeastern Wyoming got its start as a railroad terminal in 1891. A vital part of the coal-mining industry today, Gillette also has a vibrant commercial center that offers recreational activities such as golfing, mine tours, and rodeo-related events.

5. Rock Springs: population 23,036

Known as the home of fifty-six nationalities, Rock Springs is one of Wyoming's most diverse cities. Nearby attractions include Flaming Gorge National Recreation Area and the Wild Horse Scenic Loop Tour, where visitors can view large wild horse herds.

WYOMING ★ ★ ★ ★

6. Sheridan: population 17,444

Cradled by the Bighorn Mountains, this historic cowboy town was once the site where Buffalo Bill held his legendary Wild West Show. The Brinton Museum, which features Native American and Western art collections, opened in 2015.

7. Green River: population 12,515

Named for the swift-flowing, greenish river that runs through it, this city is vital to the trona mining industry. A splash park and a historic walking path are among Green River's many attractions.

8. Evanston: population 12,359

This city in southwestern Wyoming was founded as a railroad town in 1868. Today, its beautiful mountain setting attracts outdoor enthusiasts who come to camp, hike, fish, and ride mountain bikes. Evanston is also a commercial and shipping center.

9. Riverton: population 10,615

Nicknamed "The Rendezvous City," Riverton is located along the Big Wind River in a successful agricultural area. Popular festivals include the Hot Air Balloon Rally and the Wild West Winter Carnival. The Wind River **Casino** is just outside town.

10. Jackson: population 9,577

This nature-lover's paradise is named after mountain man, trapper, and trader David Jackson. Skiing is the big draw here all winter, but people come year-round to view the diverse wildlife, from the many bird species to elk and deer.

Sheridan

Jackson

Around the same time, a treaty was signed with the Shoshone at Fort Bridger. The Shoshone, under the leadership of Chief Washakie, were granted a 2.2 million-acre (890,300 ha) reservation in the Wind River Valley. There was peace between the whites and Native Americans, but it was only temporary.

Gold and the Railroad

By about 1865, fewer than one thousand white people were living in the Wyoming region. Most settled around Fort Laramie and Fort Bridger. However, with the discovery of gold at South Pass in 1867, things changed. Thousands of prospectors and fortune-seekers moved into the surrounding area. They established several mining camps, one of which became South Pass City. Within a short time, the town had nearly four thousand residents.

Ride 'em Cowboys

In 2003, Wyoming designated rodeo as the state's official sport.

That same year, construction of the Union Pacific Railroad reached southern Wyoming. This project was designed to span the entire United States and its territories from east to west. Coal was discovered along the railroad line. It was mined to fuel the trains once construction was completed.

A hotel for weary travelers in Laramie was built close to the new railroad tracks.

Several towns, including Cheyenne, were established close to the mines. Cheyenne became the Union Pacific's first terminal—or stop—in Wyoming. Just months later, Cheyenne was a bustling city with close to six thousand residents. Most residents were railroad workers.

Other towns that sprang up along the railroad line were Laramie, Rawlins, Rock Springs, Green River, Evanston, Benton, Bryan, and Bear River City. By the time the railroad was completed, Wyoming's population had grown from one thousand to eleven thousand.

The Wyoming Territory

As the population started soaring in the late 1860s, residents wanted to become part of a separate territory. At the time, the land that includes present-day Wyoming was part of the huge Dakota Territory, which was organized in 1861. Decision-makers in Washington, DC, listened. On July 25, 1868, the Wyoming Organic Act was passed. The Wyoming Territory was cut from the western portion of the Dakota Territory. The following year, President Ulysses S. Grant appointed Brigadier General John A. Campbell as the territory's first governor. Cheyenne was chosen as territorial capital.

Ranching

Numerous cattle ranches sprang up in Wyoming during the 1870s. Grazing land in Wyoming was good, especially in the territory's eastern section. Cattle were driven from Wyoming's plains to railroad terminals like Cheyenne and then shipped to market. Throughout the 1870s, cattlemen built huge ranches in Wyoming. These ranchers became very wealthy and powerful. A group of these cattle barons formed the Wyoming Stock Growers Association in 1879. This powerful association's members were often able to persuade the territorial legislature to pass laws that protected their land and business interests.

However, small ranchers also lived in Wyoming, and they were denied membership in the Wyoming Stock Growers Association. Many smaller ranchers found themselves disagreeing with the association's members. Small ranchers tended to put up fences around their land to prevent neighboring cattle from entering their animals' grazing

Footsteps of Giants

At Red Gulch Dinosaur Tracksite, located near the community of Shell, visitors can see dinosaur footprints from around 167 million years ago.

A conflict between small and wealthy cattle farmers called the Johnson County War was turned into a movie.

areas. Large ranchers preferred the fenceless, open-range grazing method. There were often clashes between the two groups.

Sheep ranches were also popping up in the territory. Wyoming's cattle ranchers often fought with the sheep ranchers. Cattle ranchers were unhappy that the sheep chewed the grass down to the ground, ruining the cattle's grazing land.

Beginning in the mid-1880s, things started to go badly for ranchers. At that time, close to one million cattle were grazing on Wyoming's rich prairie grasses. The prairies became severely overgrazed. A major drought hit the territory during the summer of 1886, drying up much of the land. A few months after that, a bitter-cold winter struck. The combination of both extreme weather conditions in less than a year took its toll on Wyoming's cattle, causing huge losses, particularly for the large, open-range ranchers.

In 1892, some of Wyoming's cattle barons hired Texas gunmen to round up small ranchers whom they thought were stealing cattle. They surrounded a cabin near the town of Buffalo, killing two men in the cabin. Furious local citizens went after the gunmen. President Benjamin Harrison sent in federal troops to resolve the issue and to reestablish order. The event became known as the Johnson County War.

Wyoming Becomes A State

Between 1880 and 1890, Wyoming's population more than tripled, growing from 20,789 to 62,555. Because it was growing so rapidly, many Wyoming residents and lawmakers felt it was time for the territory to become a state. In 1888, the territorial legislature drew up and signed a petition, asking to be admitted into the Union. Its members then sent the petition to the US Congress in Washington, DC.

Women were given the right to vote in Wyoming when it became a territory in 1869. Women in the United States couldn't vote for another 51 years.

The following year, fifty-five Wyoming **delegates** gathered in Cheyenne to create a state constitution. They discussed various issues, including judges' salaries, the marking of county lines, and women's voting rights. The US Congress ratified the constitution that the Wyoming delegates had drafted. On July 10, 1890, Wyoming became the forty-fourth state in the Union.

By the time Wyoming was admitted into the Union, other industries besides ranching were important in the state's growth. Close to two thousand laborers worked in Wyoming's coal mines. The majority of Wyoming's miners were immigrants from Great Britain, Sweden, and China.

Oil also played an important role in Wyoming's growth. In 1883, the territory's first oil well was put in place at Dallas Dome in Fremont County. Eleven years later, the city of Casper established an oil **refinery**, where oil could be processed. At first, Wyoming's oil was used mostly to fuel the Union Pacific Railroad's trains. However, with the invention of the automobile in the early 1900s, the state's oil had new uses. Wyoming's oil industry began to make a lot of money. Many workers rushed in looking for jobs in the state's numerous oil fields.

Farming wasn't well established in Wyoming before statehood because most of the region was too dry to grow corn or vegetables. That began to change when the US Bureau of Reclamation was established in the early 1900s. The bureau authorized six dam and reservoir projects along the North Platte River. These projects brought irrigation to Fremont County and to Cody and Powell in the Bighorn Basin. With a plentiful supply of underground water, Wyoming's agricultural production began to steadily increase.

World War I and the Great Depression

In 1917, the United States entered World War I. Close to twelve thousand Wyomingites—roughly 7 percent of the population—reported for active duty. Wyoming's oil was in very high demand to fuel the US Army's tanks and military vehicles overseas during the war.

After the war ended in 1918, the United States entered a period of prosperity. Some people had extra money to spend. Many began taking car trips on the country's new roads and highways. Popular destinations in Wyoming included Yellowstone National Park, Devils Tower (the country's first national monument), and the area that became Grand Teton National Park in 1929.

People employed by the Works Progress Administration during the Great Depression often lived in tent cities near forests.

The boom experienced during the 1920s ended with a bust. In 1929, the Great Depression hit. Like other Americans, Wyomingites faced hard times. Banks and stores across the country closed. Agricultural and fuel prices dropped, causing many workers to lose their jobs. Some of Wyoming's mines closed. Many people could not make a living.

In 1941, the United States entered World War II. The war helped Wyoming recover from the effects of the Great Depression. The state's oil refineries resumed production to help power US trains, tanks, and airplanes both at home and overseas. The state's cattle industry also improved, as large amounts of beef were needed to feed the military.

The 310,000 acres (125,450 ha) of the Grand Teton National Park allow for camping, hiking, boating, and other activities.

Many factories around the United States were operating day and night to produce goods for the war effort. These factories employed many Americans. The factories needed more coal to keep their machinery running. For that reason, Wyoming's coal mines were reopened. The state produced about 6 million tons (5.4 million t) of coal each year during the course of the war.

After the War and into the Future

Wyoming's energy and mineral industries continued to grow after World War II. More oil was discovered in the Bighorn Basin and in northeastern Wyoming. In addition, trona—a mineral used in the making of glass, paper, soap, and baking soda—was found in the Green River Basin in 1947. Mining operations developed in that area. The Green River region came to be known as the "Trona Capital of the World."

World War II had increased demand for very powerful weapons, such as nuclear (atomic) weapons. Uranium, a natural element found mostly underground, was needed to manufacture these weapons. In 1951, uranium was discovered in Wyoming's Powder River area. For a few years, Wyoming experienced a uranium boom similar to the oil boom.

Wyoming's oil industry received a boost in the 1970s when the United States was confronted with a serious oil shortage. The state's oil refineries were very productive.

Old Faithful is the most famous of the many geysers that spray water and steam into the air above Yellowstone National Park.

Wyoming's population continued to increase, in part due to the jobs created by the state's successful oil industry. The state's population soared by 42 percent between 1970 and 1980.

However, change came to Wyoming when worldwide oil prices began to drop in the mid-1980s. This forced Wyoming's oil companies to reduce production. In addition, many countries signed an agreement to limit the number of nuclear weapons in the world. This stopped Wyoming's uranium mining. Because of these developments, thousands of Wyomingites lost their jobs. Between 1980 and 1990, the state's population fell by 15,969.

In 1988, Yellowstone National Park was struck by a series of destructive wildfires. The number of tourists visiting Wyoming dropped significantly. Many people who worked in the tourism industry (hotel workers, tour guides, etc.) lost their jobs.

After these misfortunes, Wyoming showed an amazing ability to recover. Beginning in the 1990s, Wyoming's coal, oil, and natural gas production has steadily increased. A law was passed requiring out-of-state corporations to pay a special tax on minerals taken from Wyoming's mines. This money has helped the state's cities, schools, and highways. The fire-damaged areas of Yellowstone are slowly recovering. The tourism industry has improved as visitors come back to the state. In light of these positive developments, Wyoming's future indeed looks quite bright.

10 KEY DATES IN STATE HISTORY

1. Around 10,000 BCE

The Clovis people are some of the earliest humans to live in present-day Wyoming.

2. 1400-1500 CE

The Shoshone Native Americans travel from the west and north through the Big Horn, Powder, and Tongue Basins, arriving in the area now known as Wyoming.

3. 1812

Robert Stuart, a trapper with John Jacob Astor's American Fur Company, discovers a pass through the Rocky Mountains. It becomes known as South Pass.

4. December 10, 1869

Wyoming women are given the right to vote and to hold office on an equal basis with men.

5. March 1, 1872

Yellowstone National Park, the first national park in the world, is established and opened to the public. President Ulysses S. Grant's Yellowstone Act of 1872 designated this region as a "public park … for the benefit and enjoyment of the people."

6. July 10, 1890

President Benjamin Harrison signs a bill into law making Wyoming the forty-fourth state in the Union.

7. January 5, 1925

After an emergency election following the death of her husband (and governor) William B. Ross, Nellie Tayloe Ross becomes Wyoming's governor and the first female governor in the United States.

8. June-November 1988

Wildfires burn huge areas in and around Yellowstone National Park, damaging over 1 million acres (404, 685 ha).

9. April 10, 2013

Twenty counties are declared natural disaster areas after drought conditions make 2012 the driest period in 118 years.

10. September 23, 2014

A federal judge reinstates protection for wolves in Wyoming under the Endangered Species Act. Hunters had killed sixty-two wolves in the first year after this federal protection was lifted in 2012.

A barrel racer competes at the Frontier Days rodeo in Cheyenne.

3

The People

The area that is Wyoming today has been home to people for many thousands of years. From the earliest Native Americans to today's residents, Wyomingites have their own way of looking at the world. Wyoming is unique among America's fifty states because it has so much open space. The people of the Equality State value this vastness. Writers from Patricia MacLachlan to Nathaniel Burt have prized Wyoming's open lands in their works. Does that mean that everyone in Wyoming lives in a cabin in the middle of nowhere? Absolutely not.

The Equality State is home to people from all walks of life. However, whether they are city or country dwellers, Wyomingites tend to have an intense respect for the land. Many celebrate Wyoming's scenery and open vistas. People work and play on the land, from the Grand Tetons to the green spaces of Wyoming's urban areas.

Keeping Wyoming's land as natural as possible is a priority for many Wyomingites. In fact, nearly half of the state's land is owned by the US government. But this doesn't mean that no one can use the state- or federal-owned land. Wyomingites and people from around the globe come to enjoy much of this protected land—whether in the form of national parks, national wildlife refuges, or national monuments. Numerous Wyomingites question any land development projects that could threaten forests, mountains, or plains, or the animals that live in those areas.

In 2001, Governor Dave Freudenthal signed into law a bill creating a trust fund to preserve and to restore Wyoming's wildlife habitat. The Wyoming Game and Fish Department describes its vision as "dedicated to the conservation of sustainable, functional ecosystems capable of supporting wildlife populations at least as healthy, abundant, and diverse as they were at the dawn of the twenty-first century." These could be seen as two modern-day examples showing how the overwhelming majority of Wyomingites still value the land and the environment. But residents of the Equality State also believe in developing new industries and businesses, so long as these new endeavors are in line with taking care of the land and all its beauty.

Wyoming was once a remote frontier outpost with little connection to the busy states and cities in the east. Its early fur-trapping and trading "mountain men" were largely cut off from the rest of the world because they worked in very isolated areas. Even in the remote parts of Wyoming, this isolation is no longer a reality. Due to advances in technology, communications, and transportation, people living in the Equality State are connected to the world at large.

Despite its large land area, Wyoming has the smallest total population of any state in the Union. Some cities in the United States, such as Seattle, Washington, have more residents than the entire state of Wyoming. Wyoming's cities are not heavily populated when compared to cities in other states. Many communities and towns are spread out. As a result, Wyoming ranks forty-ninth among the fifty states when it comes to population density. (Only Alaska has a lower population density than Wyoming.) Population density refers to the number of people living within an area, such as the number of people living in each square mile (2.6 sq km) of land. On average, fewer than six people live on each square mile (2.6 sq km) of Wyoming land.

Horse Power

Wyoming's license plates feature a horse named Old Steamboat.

Wyoming's population is spread out, but that does not mean that everybody lives on a ranch, farm, or any other large piece of land out in the countryside. In fact, more than half of all Wyomingites are classified as urban dwellers. The US Census Bureau—the government agency that collects information about the country's population and economy—defines urban dwellers as people who live in towns or cities of 2,500 people or more. The majority of Wyomingites live in the southern portion of the state along Interstate 80 and the Union Pacific railroad line.

In Wyoming—as in all states—more people live in the cities or towns with more job opportunities. Some live in bustling apartment buildings, others in quiet residential neighborhoods. People might commute to work along a major highway or take public transit to their destination. Teens might go to the movies or shop at the mall for fun on the weekends. Life in Wyoming's cities is similar to life in many other cities around the United States.

The streets of Cheyenne can be busy, but Wyoming is one of the least-crowded states in the country.

With a population of about sixty thousand, Cheyenne, the state's capital, is the largest city in Wyoming. Located in the southeastern corner of the state, Cheyenne is a major commercial, industrial, and transportation center. Much of Wyoming's banking, governmental affairs, and other business deals take place here. But Cheyenne is also a city steeped in culture. The museums here, such as the Wyoming State Museum and the Old West Museum, offer visitors and locals alike the chance to learn about the history, wildlife, and natural resources of the Equality State. Events in Cheyenne, including the Frontier Days celebration, also **commemorate** Wyoming's pioneer history. Music lovers can attend concerts by the Cheyenne Symphony Orchestra. Nature lovers might enjoy visiting the city's beautifully maintained botanical gardens. Cheyenne offers activities for people with all different interests.

The next largest city, with over fifty-five thousand people, is Casper. This city is Wyoming's oil capital and chief manufacturing center. It's also home to Fort Caspar, a reconstructed 1865 military post located at an important river crossing. (The fort is named for Lt. Caspar Collins, who was killed by Cheyenne warriors in 1865. The fort was

Who Wyomingites Are

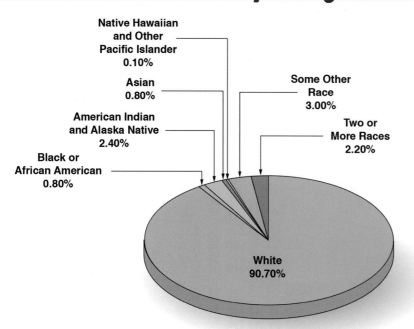

Native Hawaiian and Other Pacific Islander
0.10%

Asian
0.80%

American Indian and Alaska Native
2.40%

Black or African American
0.80%

Some Other Race
3.00%

Two or More Races
2.20%

White
90.70%

Total Population
563,626

Hispanic or Latino (of any race):
• 50,231 people (8.9%)

Note: The pie chart shows the racial breakdown of the state's population based on the categories used by the US Bureau of the Census. The Census Bureau reports information for Hispanics or Latinos separately, since they may be of any race. Percentages in the pie chart may not add to 100 because of rounding.

Source: US Bureau of the Census, 2010 Census

named in honor of the fallen lieutenant but originally those doing so misspelled his first name and called it Fort Casper. The fort, which was rebuilt in 1936 and renamed correctly, is now owned and operated by the city of Casper. The misspelling was repeated when the city was founded in 1889, and it was never corrected.) This crossing was used by people traveling the Oregon Trail and on the Pony Express route (among other trails). The Bureau of Land Management also runs the excellent National Historic Trails Interpretive Center in Casper. Here, people can learn all about the native cultures in this area, as well as how people used the various trails during the period of westward expansion. Today, local snowboarders and skiers can enjoy winter activities at Hogadon Ski Area, which is just twenty minutes from downtown Casper at Casper Mountain.

With nearly thirty-one thousand residents, Laramie is the state's third-largest city. It was named after Jacques LaRamie, one of the first white men to come to Wyoming as a fur trapper. Today, Laramie is the home of the University of Wyoming, which is known for its outstanding **geology** and art museums. Wyoming does not have any major league sports teams of its own. However, Wyomingites enjoy cheering for the various University of Wyoming Cowboys teams. The Equality State also is home to a number of minor league sports teams, including the Laramie Colts (baseball), Wyoming Knights (football), Cheyenne Grizzlies (baseball), and the Yellowstone Quake (hockey).

Though their populations are smaller, other cities are important centers for Wyoming's mining and agricultural businesses. Rock Springs, Gillette, and Sheridan each have populations between seventeen thousand and thirty-one thousand residents. Wyoming also has many small communities. Some are not even called towns. Instead the US Census data describes these locations as "census-designated places." It is not unusual for some of these communities to have populations of fewer than fifty people!

Wyomingites

More than 90 percent of Wyomingites are white. Many of them are the descendants of the state's early English, German, and Irish settlers who came to the territory in the late nineteenth century. Most of these settlers started out as cattle ranchers, sheepherders, or farmers.

Throughout Wyoming's history, a variety of other immigrant groups have also made their way into the state. For example, many Scandinavians settled in eastern Wyoming's farming areas. German, Russian, and Mexican immigrants were also drawn to the agricultural areas in the North Platte Valley and Bighorn Basin, where many of these immigrants prospered growing sugar beets. However, not all immigrants who came to Wyoming worked the land as farmers or ranchers. People from Greece, Italy, Slovakia, and Finland were among those who showed up to work in Wyoming's coal mines, particularly in the areas around Sheridan and Rock Springs. Some of these immigrants also worked in the state's gold mines.

Chinese immigrants also came to Wyoming to work on the railroads or in the mines. Some of these laborers were brought to Wyoming in the 1800s, though they didn't all stay. Riots against them as well as anti-Asian immigration policies later in the 1800s drove many Asian workers out of Wyoming. As immigration policies shifted after World War II, some Asian people came to Wyoming. But even today less than 1 percent (0.8 percent) of Wyoming's population is of Asian background.

As far back as 1870, jobs attracted African Americans to Wyoming. Railroad construction and mining jobs were of particular interest since they paid well. Even back in the early 1900s, African Americans added to the richness in communities such as Laramie, Rock Springs, Sheridan, and Cheyenne (among others). Laramie County was home to William Jefferson Hardin, the first African American to serve on a legislative assembly in the state. He served in the territorial legislature from 1879 to 1882. Today, African Americans make up about 0.8 percent of the population.

10 KEY PEOPLE ★ ★ ★

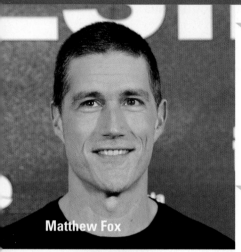
Matthew Fox

Jesse Garcia

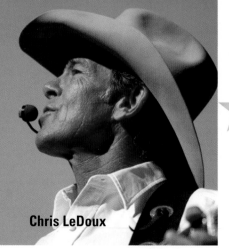
Chris LeDoux

1. Buffalo Bill Cody

At age fourteen, William Frederick "Buffalo Bill" Cody was a rider for the Pony Express. He later made headlines for his hunting ability. In the 1890s, Buffalo Bill became famous for his traveling Wild West show featuring staged battles between cowboys and Native Americans.

2. Matthew Fox

Matthew Fox was born in Pennsylvania, but moved to the Wind River Indian Reservation when he was just a year old. Fox has starred on television series such as *Party of Five* and *Lost*, and in the 2013 film *World War Z*.

3. Jesse Garcia

Winner of the ALMA (American Latino Media Arts) award, actor Jesse Garcia was born in Rawlins in 1982. Among his movie credits are *The Avengers* and *Alexander and the Terrible, Horrible, No Good, Very Bad Day*.

4. Curt Gowdy

Born in Green River, Curt Gowdy was a leading American sportscaster, covering events from the Olympic Games to the Super Bowl. An avid fisherman, he hosted *American Sportsman* and won thirteen Emmy Awards.

5. Chris LeDoux

Chris LeDoux competed in the rodeo circuit in the 1960s and 1970s. He became a well-known and respected bareback rider. However, LeDoux always loved writing and playing music and became famous for his country songs about rodeo life, cowboys, and the West.

WYOMING ★ ★ ★ ★

6. Esther Hobart Morris

In 1870, the voters of South Pass City elected Esther Hobart Morris to the position of justice of the peace. She was the first female judge in the United States. She tried dozens of cases during her time in this position.

7. Patricia MacLachlan

Ever since her childhood in Wyoming, author Patricia MacLachlan said she felt a connection to the wide-open prairie. Her children's books, including *Sarah, Plain and Tall* and *Skylark*, reflect this connection to the landscape.

Patricia MacLachlan

8. Jackson Pollock

Born in Cody in 1912, Jackson Pollock was a painter. He was known for his experimental style of **abstract** art, particularly his "drip style" technique where he used trowels, sticks, and even knives to splatter paint all over his canvases.

9. Nellie Tayloe Ross

Trained as a kindergarten teacher, Nellie Tayloe Ross was elected Wyoming's governor in 1924. She was America's first female governor. She later became director of the US Mint, the government agency in charge of producing and distributing coins.

Nellie Tayloe Ross

10. Washakie

Washakie was a Shoshone warrior and chief of the Eastern Band of the Shoshone living in Wyoming. Washakie negotiated a treaty with the US government that allowed the building of railroads through Shoshone lands and maintained peace between the settlers and the Native Americans.

Washakie

Basque immigrants came to Wyoming to use their skills herding sheep and goats.

Nearly 9 percent of the state's residents are of Hispanic or Latino heritage. Some of Wyoming's Hispanic residents are descendants of Basque sheepherders who came to the state toward the end of the nineteenth century. The Basques are from the Pyrenees Mountain region of Spain and France, where they are known for their skills at herding sheep and goats. Many Basques moved to Wyoming because they saw similarities between the state's plains and those of their homeland. Other Hispanic Wyomingites also migrated here from Texas and New Mexico, especially as migrant farm workers. In the town of Rock Springs, Hispanics make up 16 percent of the population. Many of these immigrants come from Mexico and work in the natural gas fields. Others run bakeries, **taquerías** (taco shops), and other businesses. The Hispanic population is growing the fastest of any minority group in Wyoming.

Native Americans

Before any white explorers or settlers arrived, Native Americans were the only ones living in the region. Today, however, they make up only about 2.4 percent of the state's total population. The largest Native American groups within the state are the Arapaho and the Shoshone.

There are Native Americans living in the towns and cities of Wyoming. However, nearly all of the Northern Arapaho and Eastern Shoshone live on more than 2 million acres (809,371 ha) of reservation land called the Wind River Indian Reservation. Located in southwestern Wyoming near the city of Lander, it is the seventh-largest Native American reservation in the United States. The Arapaho live in the southern section of the reservation. They have settlements at Ethete, Arapahoe, and St. Stephens. The Shoshone make their homes on the reservation's northern, western, and south-central portions. The Shoshone's major settlements are at Fort Washakie, Crowheart, and Wind River.

Both Native groups own most of the reservation land, some of which contains coal, oil, and natural gas. If the tribes allow a petroleum, natural gas, or mining company to use the resources from the area, that company must pay the Native Americans a royalty. This means that the Native Americans receive a share of the money that is made when coal, oil, and natural gas is taken from their land and sold.

Arapaho youths practice their archery skills on the Wind River Indian Reservation.

Buffalo Bill Cody Stampede Rodeo

Ice-Fishing Derby

1. Buffalo Bill Cody Stampede Rodeo

This four-day rodeo, held in Cody, recreates the level of excitement and drama that marked Buffalo Bill's original Wild West shows. In addition to riding and roping activities, there are rodeo entertainers, parades, and clowns.

2. Cheyenne Celtic Musical Arts Festival

This event, held in June at the Cheyenne Depot Museum, celebrates the Irish heritage of many Wyoming residents. There is a parade, music, pipe bands, Irish step dancing, a fiddle contest, and the "Calling of the Clans."

3. Cinco de Mayo Fiesta

This festival is held on the first Saturday in May in Evanston. Events include a community pride parade, a tortilla-eating contest, a Mexican yell (or grita) contest, and a piñata-breaking contest. Mariachi bands, traditional dancing, and fireworks add to the festivities.

4. Gold Rush Days

Each July, South Pass City celebrates Wyoming's mining history with Gold Rush Days. Events include a mining contest in which contestants drill holes into solid rock with traditional tools. Children can also pan for gold in Willow Creek.

5. Ice-Fishing Derby

Held at Saratoga Lake each January, this event challenges participants to brave the freezing cold and compete for cash prizes. There are even prizes awarded for the best hut or fishing shelter, and the best fish story.

WYOMING ★ ★ ★ ★

6. Indian Sun Dances

Each July, Wyoming's Eastern Shoshone and Northern Arapaho participate in various Sun dances, which are ancient spiritual rituals. The Sun dances are held on the Wind River Indian Reservation.

7. Jackson Hole Fall Arts Festival

Jackson Hole's arts festival showcases visual arts, such as sculpture, pottery, and painting; performing arts, such as music; and culinary arts, such as cooking and baking. The festival also celebrates folk art and Native American arts and crafts.

8. River Festival

This two-day festival is held in Green River in mid-August. This family-friendly event features activities including the Run With the Horses marathon, a car show, a hula-hoop contest, fireworks, and the Great Duck Race.

9. Woodchopper's Jamboree and Rodeo

Each Father's Day weekend, loggers from around the country come to Encampment to compete for the title of Rocky Mountain Champion Lumberjack. Participants race to chop logs and saw square blocks in half using saws or axes.

10. Wyoming State Fair

The Wyoming State Fair is held every August in Douglas. In addition to livestock shows, there are creative exhibits that include a best hobby collection, 4-H technology division display, and projects done by local Scout troops.

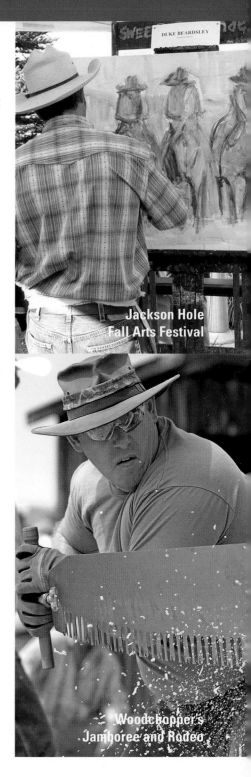

Jackson Hole Fall Arts Festival

Woodchopper's Jamboree and Rodeo

A statue of Esther Hobart Morris, the first woman elected to a public position in the United States, stands in front of the capitol building.

How the Government Works

Before Wyoming had a territorial legislature, life was sometimes dangerous for its residents. After all, boomtowns such as Laramie and Cheyenne were home to outlaws and others who took the law into their own hands. Getting people to settle disputes fairly and honestly was a real challenge in the early days when railroads were being built in what is now Wyoming.

True law and order and better cooperation among its citizens began in earnest when Wyoming's first territorial legislature met on October 12, 1869. At this session, a lawmaker from South Pass City named William Bright proposed an idea that surprised many. Bright suggested that women be given the right to vote and to hold office on an equal basis with men. At that time, men in the Wyoming territory outnumbered women six to one. Leaders hoped that such a progressive law might encourage more women to settle there. The Wyoming legislature saw the wisdom in embracing such a revolutionary concept, and on December 10, 1869, it became a law. This was the first law of its kind in the United States. When Wyoming later became a state, it was—and still is—known as the Equality State.

Wyoming's voters did not waste any time putting the new law into practice. On February 17, 1870, just two months after Bright's bill was passed, the voters of South Pass

Louisa Ann Swain is remembered in a statue at the Wyoming House for Historic Women.

City elected Esther Hobart Morris to serve as justice of the peace. It marked the first time in the United States that a woman had been elected to such a position. Another example of women's equality in Wyoming happened in Laramie in March 1870. For the first time, the town allowed women to perform jury duty in its district courts. On September 6, 1870, Louisa Ann Swain became the first woman in the United States to vote in a general election. Today, a statue commemorating her vote stands in front of the Wyoming House for Historic Women, in Laramie.

Delegates from across the Wyoming territory gathered in Cheyenne in September 1889. Their goal was to draft a state constitution. This document set out to make clear the basic beliefs and laws of Wyoming that establish both the powers and duties of the government. A constitution also guarantees certain rights to the people living in a place (such as the Wyoming Territory). Forty-five delegates signed this new constitution, and on November 5, 1889, voters approved it as well. When the US Congress admitted Wyoming as the forty-fourth state to our union, this constitution became the highest-ranking law in the new state. Wyoming's state constitution can be changed if two-thirds of the state legislature and a majority of voters in the state approve of the changes.

Local Government

Public officials in Wyoming define a city as a community with a population of at least 4,000 residents. A town has between 150 and 4,000 residents. Wyoming has more than 100 cities

Short Tenure

Francis E. Warren served as Wyoming's first state governor for less than fifty days. He was elected by the state legislature to become the first US senator from Wyoming in 1890 and served in that role until he died in 1929.

and towns. Most of the state's cities elect a mayor and a city council. The cities and towns are grouped according to location to form counties. A county board of commissioners governs each one of Wyoming's twenty-three counties. There are three to five commissioners on each board, and they are elected to four-year terms. In addition to the county commissioners, other elected Wyoming county officials include county clerks, treasurers, and sheriffs.

Branches of Government

On a statewide level, a governor who is elected to a four-year term heads Wyoming. The state also has representatives at the national level. Voters elect two members to the US Senate in Washington, DC, and one member to the US House of Representatives.

Executive

Wyoming's executive branch is charged with making sure that the state's laws are carried out. A governor, who is elected to a four-year term, heads this branch. The governor also appoints officials who oversee different departments, including Agriculture, Game and Fish, Travel and Tourism, and Transportation. Other members of the executive branch are the secretary of state, auditor, treasurer, and superintendent of public instruction. Like the governor, each of these people is elected to a four-year term.

Legislative

Wyoming's legislative branch is in charge of making or changing the state's laws. It is divided into two houses, called the senate and the house of representatives. Legislators may put forward suggestions for new laws and also suggest changes to older laws. The state Senate has thirty members, called senators, who are elected to four-year terms. The state House of Representatives has sixty members, who are elected to two-year terms. The lawmaking and budget sessions of Wyoming's legislature cannot go longer than sixty working days over a two-year period. This is shorter than the legislative session of most other states. Some people believe that this shorter session is in line with many Wyoming citizens' desire to keep government at more of a minimum. If Wyoming's governor does not want a law to be enacted, he or she can **veto** it. This can be overturned if two-thirds of Wyoming's legislators vote to override the veto.

The legislature meets for sixty days over a two-year period in the state capitol.

WYOMING STATE CAPITOL

Judicial

The judicial branch of Wyoming's state government is a court system that is responsible for interpreting the laws that the state's legislature passes. Wyoming's highest court is the state Supreme Court. It has five justices who serve eight-year terms and are appointed by the governor. The state Supreme Court also makes decisions about whether certain laws violate Wyoming's state constitution. In addition to its Supreme Court, Wyoming has nine district courts, each of which has one or two judges appointed by the governor. These district courts deal with civil and criminal trials. The Equality State also has police courts, municipal courts, and justice of the peace courts.

How a New Law Is Created

When a law is proposed, it is called a bill. As in other states, bills in Wyoming are often written and proposed in response to the concerns of everyday citizens. After a bill is introduced, it is given to a standing committee in the state senate or house of representatives. There, it is considered and discussed by the members of the committee. The committee then votes on the bill to give it a "pass" or "do not pass" recommendation. If the committee passes the bill, it will be discussed and debated by members of that house. After the bill is discussed, debated, and possibly changed, the members of that chamber take a vote. If enough members vote for the bill, it goes to the other chamber. The second house discusses, debates, and votes on the bill. If it passes in the second house without any amendments, or changes, being attached to it, it is immediately sent to the governor to be signed into law. If the second house amends the bill, however, it is sent back to the first house to determine whether the members of the first house agree with the amendments. If they do not agree, the bill is given to a conference committee to iron out the differences and to reach a compromise. The conference committee then writes a report on the bill, which is again voted on by both houses.

If both houses pass the bill, it is sent to the governor for his or her final review. If the governor signs the bill, it becomes law. If the governor vetoes, or rejects, the bill, the two houses can vote again. If there are enough votes in both houses, the bill will be passed.

POLITICAL FIGURES
FROM WYOMING

Liz Byrd: Wyoming Legislator, 1981-1993

In addition to teaching elementary school for nearly forty years, Liz Byrd worked to support laws improving child safety and better pay for teachers. She also established Equality Day in Wyoming. Byrd was the first African-American woman to serve in the Wyoming legislature.

Dick Cheney: Vice President of the United States, 2001-2009

Following his graduation from the University of Wyoming, Dick Cheney held a number of governmental jobs, including US congressman and White House Chief of Staff from 1975 to 1977. As Secretary of Defense, he directed two military campaigns: Operation Just Cause in Panama and Operation Desert Storm in the Middle East.

Francis E. Warren: US Senator, 1890-1929

Francis E. Warren was a successful businessman in the state before becoming the governor of Wyoming Territory (1885–1886, 1889–1890) and the first governor of the state (1890). He was instrumental in getting Cheyenne its first lighting system. In the Senate, he worked on legislation related to the military, Native American affairs, forestry, and livestock. He was a strong supporter of women's suffrage.

WYOMING
YOU CAN MAKE A DIFFERENCE

Contacting Lawmakers

If there is something you feel strongly about in your community or your state, you can try contacting one of Wyoming's governmental officials.

To contact the governor, **visit governor.wyo.gov/contact-us**. You will see a form where you can e-mail Wyoming's governor directly or an address where you can send your question or comment.

To contact one of your state representatives or senators, visit **legisweb.state.wy.us/ LegislatorSummary/LegislatorList.aspx**. On the left-hand side of the page, click on either the tab that says House Members or the tab that says Senate Members. A list of all the state officials and e-mail contacts will appear.

To learn the name of your state representative, visit **legisweb.state.wy.us**. Click on Locate Your Representative and choose the link near the top of the screen that says Find Your District. You then can enter your home address. Congressmen can be found at: **www.govtrack.us/ congress/members/WY**

Tracking Fracking

Hydraulic fracturing (or fracking) is a process of extracting oil and gas from shale rock. Energy companies drill into the earth and inject a high-pressure water mixture into the rock to release the

> **Silly Law**
>
> It's illegal to spit on the steps of a school in Cheyenne.

valuable oil and gas. But the water mixture contains a number of chemicals, many of which are considered to be risky to the health of people and the environment. Prior to 2010, these energy companies did not have to disclose what chemicals they were using in the fracking process under the 2005 Energy Policy Act.

A number of individuals and organizations rallied to voice their concerns. They expressed their fears about toxic chemicals contaminating Wyoming's groundwater supplies. They demanded that energy companies be completely transparent about what chemicals were injected into which specific wells and in what concentrations. Wyoming was the first state in the country to establish such a law.

Tourism is big business in Wyoming, and the exhilarating ski area at Jackson Hole is one of the state's most popular attractions.

Making a Living

5

Wyoming is a state that is rich in many ways. To begin with, the Equality State is lucky to have many natural resources. Under Wyoming's sweeping plains and enormous mountains lie treasure in the form of coal, natural gas and oil reserves, and many other minerals. Wyoming is also fortunate to have terrific grazing lands for its herds of sheep and cattle. And of course, millions of tourists from around the globe might not flock to Wyoming if it weren't for the state's incredible scenery—from the majestic mountains of the Grand Tetons to the bubbling mud pots and geothermal wonders of Yellowstone National Park.

Of course, the industries that have helped Wyoming's economy grow and prosper have changed throughout the state's colorful history. Mining and cattle ranching were the most important industries in the late nineteenth century. Then farming took the lead during the beginning of the twentieth century. Petroleum (oil) and natural gas extraction were popular in the 1970s and 1980s. As the twenty-first century began, mining once again became one of the most important parts of Wyoming's economy. The service industry—which includes any jobs that provide a service to people—is also a key part of the state's success.

Uranium mining has gone through periods of boom and bust in Wyoming.

Mining

Mining is huge in Wyoming, making up about one-third of its gross state product, or GSP. The GSP is the value of all goods and services provided by a state during a specific time period. In 2013, 37 percent of Wyoming's total output came from its mining industry—the most of any state in America. The state's budget depends heavily on the taxes earned from extracting its mineral resources, so a bad year for the mining industry can really help or hurt the whole economy of the state. Wyoming ranks high in coal production, gas production, and petroleum extraction.

One of the state's most important minerals is natural gas, and in 2014, Wyoming produced 1.8 trillion cubic feet (50.9 billion cubic meters) of it. Most of Wyoming's natural gas production takes place in Sweetwater, Campbell, Sublette, and Fremont Counties.

Coal is another of Wyoming's most important minerals. Wyoming leads the nation in coal production, accounting for about 40 percent of all the coal mined in the United States. In 2014, Wyoming's coal mines, the majority of which are located in Campbell and Carbon Counties, produced more than 396 million tons (359 million t) of coal. All eight of the nation's largest coal mines are located within Wyoming's Powder River Basin. At Peabody Energy's North Antelope Rochelle Mine, the nation's largest coal mine, production in 2014 increased by 6 percent. Just this one mine, located 65 miles (105 km) south of Gillette, produced 118 million tons (107 million t) that year. Coal from Wyoming mines has been used to fuel power plants in more than thirty states in recent years. Wyomingites are proud of the fact that most of the state's coal is low in sulfur, a type of natural element. This helps cut down on pollution when the coal is burned as a fuel, making it very desirable.

Petroleum also plays an important part in Wyoming's economy. The state typically accounts for 2 to 3 percent of the total US crude oil production. Almost all of Wyoming's twenty-three counties produce oil, but the counties that produce the most are Park, Natrona, Campbell, Fremont, Hot Springs, and Sweetwater. Wyoming has six operating oil refineries that process diesel fuel, motor gasoline, **aviation** fuel, and other products. Two of these refineries are located near a crude oil pipeline hub in Casper.

Wyoming leads the United States in the production of trona—a grayish-yellowish mineral consisting of sodium, carbon, and water. Found deep below Earth's surface near Green River, the mineral is primarily made into sodium carbonate. This is then used to manufacture glass, pulp and paper, detergents, cosmetics, and chemicals.

Other important minerals that are native to Wyoming are agate, jade, diamonds, limestone, marble, gold, sapphires, rubies, copper, gypsum, and bentonite, a type of clay used in drilling oil wells.

Uranium, a radioactive element used in the production of nuclear energy and weapons, is also found in Wyoming. During the 1970s, the state had a booming uranium business. That came to a halt in the early 1980s because of foreign competition, and because many countries agreed to limit the production of nuclear weapons. However, increased prices for uranium have led to new uranium mining activity in recent years. Even though Wyoming itself does not have any nuclear power plants, it is a leading producer of uranium ore (used to fuel such plants).

Agriculture

Since the early twentieth century, agriculture's importance to Wyoming's economy has decreased. Of the state's 295,192 workers, only about 3,200 are involved in farming

Cattle

Coal

1. Cattle

Livestock have been a fixture on Wyoming's plains since the cattle drives of the 1870s. Most of Wyoming's agricultural income comes from the sale of beef cattle and calves.

2. Coal

Coal is one of the most important minerals in Wyoming. Coal deposits lie underneath about 40 percent of Wyoming's land. Most of the mining of the mineral takes place in the state's northeastern and south-central regions. Wyoming's mines yield more than 400 million tons (363 million t) each year.

3. Construction

Wyoming's construction industry has been growing dramatically in recent years, particularly since 1990. Projects include not only the construction of buildings (homes, office complexes), highways, and bridges but also utility systems, including pipelines related to the state's mining industries.

4. Education

From elementary teachers to lab technicians to university professors, the education field is a major employer of Wyomingites. Wyoming spends more money per student than most other states in the country.

5. Government

The federal government is one of the biggest employers in Wyoming. The US government owns a large percentage of the state's land. Federal workers hold all kinds of jobs, from national park rangers to people who deal with grazing rights on federal lands.

6. Hay

Hay is Wyoming's most valuable cash crop. The state's arid high plains and mountain valleys are excellent for producing high-quality alfalfa hay. Much of Wyoming's hay is exported for use in other states' dairy and equine industries.

7. Petroleum

Wyoming is a leader in petroleum production. The state has a lot of oil in the Powder River Basin and in southwestern Wyoming, where part of the Overthrust Belt is located. This belt is a geological formation with tremendous oil and gas reserves.

8. Sheep

Sheep are an important type of livestock for Wyoming. Many ranchers herd sheep for their meat and for their wool. Every year, the sheep are sheared and their coats are used to make fabrics and other material.

9. Sugar Beets

Sugar beets are one of Wyoming's main cash crops. Sugar beets look like dark red bulbs with very large, white roots. Eastern European immigrants first brought them to the state around the end of the 1800s. They produce sucrose, a natural sweetener.

10. Tourism

Wyoming has been a popular tourist destination since the 1870s. Visitors come to ski, hunt, and visit the state's scenic national parks, historic towns, museums, and cultural centers. In 2014, 10.1 million visitors generated about $3.3 billion for Wyoming's economy.

Petroleum

Sugar Beets

Recipe for Huckleberry Muffins

Huckleberries grow well in Wyoming's acidic mountainous soil. Follow this recipe to make some delicious huckleberry muffins. (If your local grocery store doesn't have huckleberries, you can use blueberries instead.) Be sure to have an adult help you with the oven. This recipe makes about eighteen muffins.

What You Need

½ cup butter (118 milliliters)

¾ cup sugar (177 mL)

2 eggs

1 cup (237 mL) plain yogurt

¼ cup (59 mL) sour cream

2½ cups (0.6 liters) all-purpose flour

½ teaspoon (2.5 mL) baking soda

1 tablespoon (15 mL) baking powder

¾ cup (177 mL) huckleberries

Glaze

1 cup (237 mL) powdered sugar

¼ cup (59 mL) whole milk

What To Do

- Preheat the oven to 350°F (177°C).
- In a large bowl, beat the butter and sugar together until creamy and smooth. Add one egg at a time, then add yogurt and sour cream.
- In a separate bowl, mix together flour, baking soda, and baking powder. Slowly add these dry ingredients into the liquid ingredients.
- Gently fold the berries into the batter. Pour into greased muffin tins, filling each tin about three-quarters full.
- Bake for about twenty minutes or until muffins are light golden-brown.
- Combine milk and powdered sugar in a small bowl. Drizzle this mixture over the muffins when they are still warm from the oven.

or agricultural services. Another 7,300 are employed in forestry, fishing, and hunting. However, agriculture is still a vital part of the Equality State's economy. In 2013, the value of Wyoming's agricultural sector output was $1.3 billion. Wyoming plays an important role in supplying a large amount of food to businesses and residents within the state as well as to people living in other states. Wyoming has about 11,500 farms and ranches that have an average size of 2,626 acres (1,063 ha). Wyoming ranks first in the nation in terms of how large its average farms and ranches are. The state uses about 30.2 million acres (12.2 million ha) of land for agricultural purposes.

A majority of the state's agricultural income comes from sheep and other livestock.

The largest part of the state's farm income comes from the sale of livestock and livestock products. This is mostly cattle and calves, from the Great Plains region, and sheep. Another piece of the state's income comes from the sale of feed and cash crops. Feed crops, such as alfalfa, corn, hay, and different types of meadow grasses, are used to feed livestock. By far, hay is the leading crop in Wyoming (in terms of income earned). Hay alone earned around $390 million for Wyoming in 2013. Cash crops are crops sold to food processors and to consumers in grocery stores and at other places that sell food. Cash crops grown in the Equality State include sugar beets, wheat, barley, dry beans (pinto, Great Northern, navy beans, etc.), and potatoes. Sugar beets earned $53.4 million for Wyoming in 2013, the second most **lucrative** crop after hay.

Manufacturing

Around 3.7 percent of Wyoming's workers have manufacturing-related jobs. Most of them work in chemical plants, petroleum refineries, industrial equipment factories, food processing plants, and forest product facilities. The state's manufacturing industry plays a huge role in supplying other states with the materials they need for various industries.

Casper, with its many oil refineries, is the state's leading manufacturing center. Cheyenne, Wyoming's largest city, is well known for the manufacture of flight instruments and testing equipment. Worland and Lovell host refineries that process sugar beets into beet sugar. The Star Valley is the state's dairy product capital.

Service

Service industries make up the largest piece of Wyoming's GSP. People who work in service industries provide services to individuals or groups, as opposed to making a product that can be sold. Examples of workers in the service industry include teachers, salesclerks, librarians, travel agents, doctors, real estate agents, bankers, and airline pilots. Wyoming's leading service industries deal with communications, transportation, and utilities. They range from radio stations and bus companies to electric power plants. Cheyenne, for example, is home to regional distribution centers for companies including Lowe's and Walmart. The University of Wyoming is also one of the largest employers in the Equality State.

One service industry in Wyoming that continues to grow is tourism. Visitors come to enjoy the state's outdoor attractions and to experience its culture and history. Not only is that money good for the state, but the thriving industry creates jobs for Wyomingites. Hotel workers, tour guides, national park rangers, and fly-fishing tour operators are just some examples of the types of tourist sector jobs in Wyoming. About 10.1 million overnight guests visited Wyoming in 2014, with the following sites being most popular: Yellowstone, Jackson Hole, Grand Teton, Cody, and Cheyenne. The Jackson Hole Mountain Resort has the largest vertical drop (distance from top of the highest ski run to the bottom of the hill) in the United States. On the other side of the Grand Tetons is the Grand Targhee Resort, which is one of the snowiest ski areas in the country.

Trona Trove

Wyoming has the world's largest deposit of trona. The state's mines produced over 17 million tons [15.4 million t] of trona and employed 2,313 people in 2014.

Another example of a modern tourist attraction involves the Wind River Indian Reservation. Throughout the summer, visitors are welcome to attend a number of powwows, where Native American community members gather to dance, sing, catch up with friends and family members, and enjoy other festivities. Several museums exist on the reservation where tourists can learn more

The venom of Wyoming's Midget Faded Rattlesnake is ten to thirty times stronger than that of the Prairie Rattlesnake.

about the history of Native Americans in Wyoming. In the town of Fort Washakie is the cemetery where Chief Washakie and Sacagawea (Lewis and Clark's Shoshone guide) are buried. Within the Wind River Reservation are also four casinos that are open to the public. The money that visitors spend here goes back into the Native American community.

From its geography to its history to its people, Wyoming can be characterized by its variety. What is common among most Wyomingites, however, is a spirit of individualism, friendliness, dedication, and a "can-do" attitude. These are traits that make rugged Wyoming a fascinating and attractive state with a colorful past and an extremely bright future.

Attractions such as the Jackson town square supply workers with jobs in the tourism industry.

WYOMING

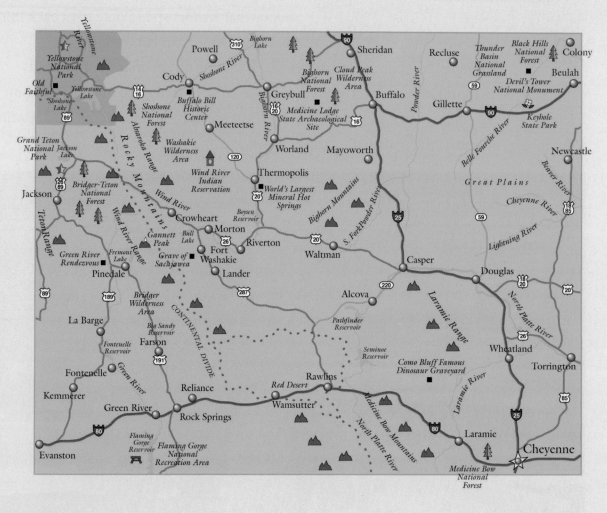

Yellowstone River

Yellowstone National Park

Old Faithful

Yellowstone Lake

Shoshone Lake

Grand Teton National Park Jackson Lake

Jackson

Teton Range

Bridger-Teton National Forest

Green River Rendezvous

Fremont Lake

Pinedale

La Barge

Fontenelle Reservoir

Fontenelle

Kemmerer

Green River

Evanston

Flaming Gorge Reservoir

Flaming Gorge National Recreation Area

Powell

Cody

Shoshone River

Buffalo Bill Historic Center

Meeteetse

Shoshone National Forest

Washakie Wilderness Area

Absaroka Range

Rocky Mountains

Wind River

Wind River Range

Gannett Peak

Grave of Sachjawea

Bull Lake

Crowheart

Morton

Fort Washakie

Lander

Bridger Wilderness Area

Big Sandy Reservoir

Farson

CONTINENTAL DIVIDE

Reliance

Green River

Rock Springs

Red Desert

Wamsutter

Bighorn Lake

Greybull

Bighorn National Forest

Cloud Peak Wilderness Area

Medicine Lodge State Archaeological Site

Worland

Thermopolis

World's Largest Mineral Hot Springs

Boysen Reservoir

Wind River Indian Reservation

Riverton

Waltman

Mayoworth

Bighorn Mountains

S. Fork Powder River

Sheridan

Buffalo

Powder River

Gillette

Recluse

Thunder Basin National Grassland

Devil's Tower National Monument

Black Hills National Forest

Colony

Beulah

Keyhole State Park

Newcastle

Great Plains

Belle Fourche River

Cheyenne River

Beaver River

Lightning River

Casper

Alcova

Pathfinder Reservoir

Seminoe Reservoir

Como Bluff Famous Dinosaur Graveyard

Rawlins

North Platte River

Laramie Range

Douglas

Wheatland

Torrington

North Platte River

Medicine Bow Mountains

Laramie River

Laramie

Cheyenne

Medicine Bow National Forest

miles
0   40

65
km

Legend

	Interstate Highway
	U.S. Highway
	State Highway
	State Capital
	City or Town
	National Forest
	Recreation Area
	State Park
	Highest Point in the State
	Mountains
	National Park
	Indian Reservation

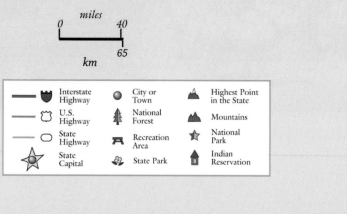

N

W   E

S

WYOMING
MAP SKILLS

1. If you drove from Casper to Torrington, which river would you cross?

2. Which national forest lies just east of Greybull?

3. Is the Red Desert east or west of the Green River?

4. Which highway would you take to drive from Evanston to Cheyenne?

5. What town lies closest to the world's largest mineral hot springs?

6. What reservoir lies southwest of Reliance?

7. Is the community of Beulah closer to Yellowstone National Park or Devils Tower National Monument?

8. In which direction would you travel to get from Laramie to Grand Teton National Park?

9. About how many miles apart are the cities of Buffalo and Sheridan?

10. Does Gannett Peak or Medicine Bow National Forest lie closer to Cheyenne?

10. Medicine Bow National Forest
9. About 40
8. Northwest
7. Devils Tower National Monument
6. Flaming Gorge Reservoir
5. Thermopolis
4. Interstate 80
3. East
2. Bighorn National Forest
1. North Platte River

Red Desert

Bighorn National Forest

State Flag, Seal, and Song

Wyoming's state flag, adopted in 1917, shows a white bison on a blue background. The state's seal, which is in blue and white, is featured in the center of the bison's side. A border of white within a border of red surrounds the blue background.

The state seal shows a woman holding a staff and a banner with the words "Equal Rights." On either side of the woman stands a man. One represents the livestock industry and the other symbolizes the mining industry. The words "Oil," "Mines," "Livestock," and "Grain" represent Wyoming's industries. The years 1869 and 1890 are when Wyoming organized its territorial government and when it became a state.

During the summer of 1903, a judge named Charles E. Winter composed a poem titled "Wyoming." This poem was written less than fifteen years after Wyoming became America's forty-fourth state. It celebrated the young state's natural beauty, from the snowy peaks of the Rocky Mountains to Wyoming's wildflowers, including the columbine, daisy, and rose. Winter's writing also **touted** the earnest citizens of Wyoming. In the 1920s, the director of the University of Wyoming's music department (named George Knapp) put Winter's poem to music. The "Wyoming March Song" was adopted as the state's official song in 1955. To view the lyrics, visit: **whp.state.wy.us/general.aspx**.

Glossary

abstract Using elements of form (such as line, color, or texture) without attempting to create a realistic picture.

aviation The flying or operating of aircraft.

casino A building or room used for gambling.

commemorate To celebrate a person, event, or situation by doing or building something.

delegate A person sent or authorized to represent others, particularly an elected representative sent to a conference.

geology A science that deals with the history of the Earth and its life, particularly as recorded in rocks.

geothermal Of, relating to, or using the heat of the Earth's interior.

habitat The natural home or environment of a plant, animal, or other organism.

irrigation Supplying water to crops or land to help them grow, often by means of channels.

lucrative Producing a great deal of wealth; profitable.

missionary A person who moves to new areas to spread his or her religion.

nomadic Relating to or characteristic of people who have no permanent home, who travel from place to place to hunt animals or find fresh pasture for their livestock.

refinery A building and the equipment used to remove the impurities from a substance like oil, metals, or sugar.

taquería A restaurant or stand that specializes in Mexican dishes such as tacos and burritos.

tout To promote or to make much of something.

veto The power of the head of a government to prevent a bill passed by a legislature from becoming a law.

More About Wyoming

BOOKS

Costain, Meredith. *Native Americans of the Great Plains*. Discovery Education: Ancient Civilizations. New York: PowerKids Press, 2013.

Felix, Rebecca. *What's Great About Wyoming?* Our Great States. Minneapolis, MN: Lerner Classroom, 2015.

Marsh, Carole. *I'm Reading About Wyoming*. Wyoming Experience. Peachtree City, GA: Gallopade International, 2014.

Prentzas, G.S. *Wyoming*. America the Beautiful. Danbury, CT: Children's Press, 2014.

WEBSITES

National Geographic on Wyoming
travel.nationalgeographic.com/travel/united-states/wyoming-guide

State of Wyoming Official Website
www.wyo.gov/about-wyoming

Wyoming for Kids
www.wyoming4kids.org

ABOUT THE AUTHORS

Alicia Klepeis began her career at the National Geographic Society. She is the author of numerous children's books including *Francisco's Kites*, *From Pizza to Pizza*, *The World's Strangest Foods*, and *Bizarre Things We've Called Medicine*.

Rick Petreycik has written articles on history, business, music, travel, and film for many publications. He lives with his family in Connecticut.

Index

Index

mines and mining, 36–37, 39, 41–42, 49, 66–68, **66**, 72, 76

missionary, 25, 29

Morris, Esther Hobart, 51, **56**, 58

mountains, 7–9, **9**, 12–14, 17, 46, 65
    Bighorn Mountains, 25, 33, 35
    Grand Teton Mountains, **6**, 26, 65
    Medicine Bow, 9
    Rocky Mountains, 9, 23, 28, 43, 76

National Elk Refuge, 15, **15**, 19

Native Americans, 14, 23–27, 29–33, 35–36, 43, 45, 50–53, 62

nomadic, 24, 26

oil, 9, 39–42, 47, 53, 63, 65, 67, 69, 72, 76

Old Faithful, 12, **42**

Oregon Trail, 31, **31**, 48

population, 5, 37, 39–40, 42, 46, 48–49, 52

railroads, 11, 33–37, 39, 47, 49, 51, 57

ranching, 14, 37–39, 65, 69, 71

refinery, 39

Ross, Nellie Tayloe, 43, 51, **51**

Sacagawea, 15, **25**, 28, 73

sheep, 8, 13, 18–19, 38, 52, **52**, 65, 69, 71, **71**

Shoshone (people), 15, 24, 26–28, 31, 36, 43, 51–54, 73

South Pass City, 36, 51, 55, 57

taquería, 52

tourism, 17, 42, 65, 69, 72

tout, 76

trees, 4, 17–18, **17**, 21

uranium, 41–42, 67

veto, 59, 61

wars,
    Civil, 33
    Johnson County, 38, **38**
    Red Cloud's, 32, **32**
    World War I, 40
    World War II, 41, 49

Washakie (chief), 15, 36, 51, **51**, 73

wildlife, 17–19, 45–47

Wind River Indian Reservation, **26**, 27, 50, 53, **53**, 54, 72

women's rights, 39, **39**, 43, 57–58, 62

Yellowstone National Park, 5, 12, **13**, 15–16, **15**, 19–20, 39–40, 42–43